Sola Adegun was born in London in 1967, the son of Nigerian parents who came to England in the late '50s. He has a master's in Adult, Continuing, and Community Education, achieved during his 30 years or so in the education sector. He has also been a social worker for a number of years before settling back into FE/HE, teaching health, English language/literature and math. Sola has always had an interest in writing, ever since writing a short booklet on the history of Willesden when he was 14 years old. He is a committed Christian, and this shines through in his debut publication of poems, thoughts and reflections.

I would like to thank the Windrush generation, without which we would have no second generation, such as I, to build upon their labours.

Sola Adegun

PERCEPTIONS OF A CHRISTIAN

Thoughts and Words for Reflection

AUSTIN MACAULEY PUBLISHERS
LONDON * CAMBRIDGE * NEW YORK * SHARJAH

Copyright © Sola Adegun 2025

The right of Sola Adegun to be identified as author of this work has been asserted by the author in accordance with sections 77 and 78 of the Copyright, Designs and Patents Act 1988.

All rights reserved. No part of this publication may be reproduced, stored in a retrieval system, or transmitted in any form or by any means, electronic, mechanical, photocopying, recording, or otherwise, without the prior permission of the publishers.

Any person who commits any unauthorised act in relation to this publication may be liable to criminal prosecution and civil claims for damages.

A CIP catalogue record for this title is available from the British Library.

ISBN 9781035845477 (Paperback)
ISBN 9781035845484 (ePub e-book)

www.austinmacauley.com

First Published 2025
Austin Macauley Publishers Ltd®
1 Canada Square
Canary Wharf
London
E14 5AA

Acknowledgements To Friends, Family, And Those Of The Household Of Faith, Particularly Yaw Asiyama, Who Has Been A Quiet Adviser.

Table of Contents

1. The Straight and Narrow Road	13
2. Sisters Want to Drive My Car (Drive It for Jesus)	14
3. What's Going On? / The Dark Knight of the Soul	15
4. In My Heart	17
5. You Get What You Pray	18
6. Where Is the Working Church Hero?	19
7. I Need More of You	20
8. Perceptions of A Christian	21
9. How Do You Praise the Lord?	22
10. I'm Still in God	23
11. Prayerless Nights	24
12. You Want Your Blessing (I Want Mine)	25
13. Sweetly Saved (Ballerina Girl)	26
14. I Will, I Must, I Can	27
15. Running with Horses	28
16. Before Serving God Went Out of Style	29
17. Listen to the Spirit Song	30
18. I've Seen a Rainbow	31
19. We're Not Together Now	32
20. She Prays She Prays She Prays	33
21. Don't Pray Me Down Too Soon!	34
22. I'm Not Satisfied	35
23. It's Only Prayer	36
24. Pray for Yourself	37
25. Frustration	38
26. Are You, My Friend?	39
27. Playing Church?	40
28. You're My Blessed Friend	41

29. One in A Million	42
30. (No Morning Glory) What's the Story?	43
31. Prayer Walking	44
32. Yes, No, Wait	45
33. You Don't Know Me	46
34. They Came in Through the Church Back Window	48
35. Gimme Wisdom	49

My thoughts and reflections, garnered over numerous years, concern life issues—particularly those viewed from a Christian standpoint or as I would like to say, vantage point. They include conversations and reflections about everyday situations, encompassing both real and imaginary discussions with brothers and sisters, both old and young, lovers, and friends. Some individuals described may be considered the 'everyman' of society, encountering situations to which, hopefully, we can all relate. The content includes subliminal conversations and discussions with the rich and famous, responding to their views and thoughts. The Spelling, Punctuation, and Grammar (SPAG) utilises a variety of forms: Standard English, Old English (Shakespearean), American English, and occasional 'street language'. If I spoke more languages fluently, I would use other forms, but suffice it to say, the different forms each add something distinct.

1.
The Straight and Narrow Road

Think of the words of Jesus concerning the Christian walk, if you please. Matthew 7:13,14. God gives us clear instruction as to the extent and nature of the road. Not 'Long and Winding' as Brother Paul, nor 'any road' as Brother George states. During the walk, sometimes we experience a whole range of emotions: laughter, sorrow, joy, and others. Sometimes we walk confidently, quickly, and at other times not so quickly, or even needing to stop along the way. Whatever the case, our challenge is forever striving to make it along the straight and narrow road.

The straight and narrow road, la da da da da,
Leads to a heavenly abode, la da da da da.
Room enough for two,
Jesus, let it be me and you.
Lord, lead me through that road.

The straight and narrow way, hey hey hey hey hey,
I've got to walk and pray (pray, pray, pray, pray, pray).
Room enough for two,
Jesus, let it be me and you.
Lord, lead me through today.

The straight and narrow street,
Is where you'll find my feet,
Room enough for two,
Jesus, let it be me and you,
Lord, lead me through that street.

The straight and narrow path, ha ha ha ha ha,
Is where I'll have a laugh,
Room enough for two,
Jesus, let it be me and you,
Lord, lead me on that path.

So straight and narrow is the call,
Not long and winding, Brother Paul.
And just any road, Brother George,
Could leave you stranded in a gorge.

Let me show you the road,
Let me show you which road to choose,
Let me show you which road to choose.

2.
Sisters Want to Drive My Car
(Drive It for Jesus)

I often reflect upon a portion of time when I used to drive three young girls, in particular, to various functions all over England. It was a difficult time because they often went to various church functions purely to meet with friends (boys!)—not to engage with God. As we often went out, I always wished the girls were going with the right motivations. Trying to drive my car, even though they were all under age, was one of the highlights of such excursions.

Here's a song about a car and me,
And teenage sisters I'll call one, two, and three.
They want to drive my car.

Sister one said we need to check out new scenes,
So we'd drive to Bletchley or Milton Keynes.
When we reached there, knowing the crowd gave them satisfaction,
Wish to God that Jesus was their main attraction.
They want to drive my car.

Sisters want to drive my car,
Sisters want to drive it near or drive it far,
Sisters want to drive my car,
Wish they'd drive it for Jesus.

Sister two, playing with my mobile phone, Till I
say, 'Look, honey, leave it alone'.
Sister three tells me, don't be a tease,
Wished they'd get down on their knees and give Jesus a call.

Sisters want to drive my car,
Sisters want to drive it near or drive it far,
Sisters want to drive my car,
Wish they'd drive it for Jesus.

3.
What's Going On? / The Dark Knight of the Soul

Have you ever gone through a really difficult period of life so difficult that it feels as though are looking for a black cat , in a dark room on a dark November night! So dark that it can be felt even to the penetration of the soul? Yes that's not a good place to be as all the meaningful things such as faith, love and worship, almost become unreachable and you are left in a state Brother M of saying 'What's going on?'

What's going on?
This empty feeling, so long
What's going on?
Can't make this a song
What's going on?
The fruits are all wrong
What's going on?
Can't pray so strong

What's happening to me?
I don't feel as free
What's happening to me?
I'm as blind as can be,
What's happening to me?
I continually plea
What's happening to me?
Can't anyone see?
What's happening to me

What's become of the church?
We've been left in the lurch.
What's become of the church?
Christ the head did perch
What's become of the church?
I'm trying to search
What's become of the church?
Ja, die nur weg durch
What's become of the church?

I suppose it should happen to me
After near ecstasy
What up flows must backslide
Once avoided now collides.
Becoming drier never higher years take a toll.
This is the dark Knight of the soul.

I expected the ups and downs of Christian life.
Disunity disharmony and major strife.
When one lives from the inside out.
Very quiet, not a shout not a lot to talk about.
Spiritually leaking from a spiritual hole.
This is the dark Knight of the soul.

Dark Knight of the soul, I hear you say,
Dark Knight of the soul please allow me to pray.
Dark Knight of the soul please leave me be.
Dark Knight of the soul please set me free,
Dark Knight of the soul in your funny way.
You go before the break of day

And give way to light of the soul

Light of the soul please don't be late.
Light of the soul I anticipate
For no matter how dark the night
Light of the soul will set me right.
And banished to a secondary role.
The one they called dark Knight of the soul.

4.
In My Heart

It sometimes takes a long time to understand that there are no ideal situations in which an individual can grow as a Christian. I spent much time in a church that was predominantly elderly and fairly strict in its doctrine. During my formative Christian experiences, I always thought that I could gain ultimate satisfaction if rules were changed, there was more youth, that sort of thing. As I reflect, I realise that many of my complaints have been fulfilled in the current church: there were more young people, rules were more relaxed, but there has been no fundamental difference in my outlook—that of wishing for change from external sources so I can be gratified internally. I have now come to understand that it is in our relationship with God, and in our hearts, that contentment is found. Godliness with contentment is great gain.

There are churches where I was a member,
Always wishing that I was someplace else.
And the members, that were brethren,
Never met my expectations and ideals.
Now I'm older and I'm wiser,
There's nothing to choose between then and now.
And instead of being the one that is the miser,
In my heart, I'll make the change.

Churches dominated by the elders,
Who stifle my Christian growth with so many rules.
If we had a few more youngsters,
And changed all the rules, we'd be okay.
Yet the rules have changed, and the youth are now the greater,
And still we complain—guess nothing has changed.
Hope the youth find out sooner rather than later, In our hearts, we must make the change.

Now I'm older and I'm wiser,
There's nothing to choose between then and now.
And instead of being the one that is the miser,
In my heart, I'll make a change.
If you really want to know what I am saying,
Then listen to me; I mean you well.
You'll get the answer: look to God and keep on praying,
For in your heart, you must make a change.

In your heart, you must make change.
In your church, you must make a change.
In my heart….

5.
You Get What You Pray

The Bible teaches that we should not be weary in well-doing. It also teaches us to put our prayers and requests before the Lord. I am a great believer in receiving what we have put to God in prayer, and in His good time, He will answer us: Yes, No, or Wait. During my experiences, I have learnt a lot about the nature of God. You'll never find the word 'fair' to describe God in the King James Version of the Bible, but you will find the word 'Just'. The scriptures encourage us that God is not unjust to forget our labour of love. So, let's remember, beloved children, we get back what we pray.

If we overcometh and pray on to the end,
Never to succumeth to any worldly trend,
Somewhere in the pain and tears,
I promise you today,
Never be discouraged,
We get back what we pray

God's not fair, but God is Just.
He's not good, but righteousness is a must.
If we're to see His face,
With all patience, we must run this race…
…But that's enough for now, child,
Nuff's as good as a feast.
Always meek and mild, child,
At the very least.

Someday when you're older,
Highly favoured and walking the narrow way,
Perhaps in God's true faithfulness,
You got back what you prayed.

6.
Where Is the Working Church Hero?

I'm old enough, or young enough, to remember not having central heating at home, sleeping three in a bed, and to this day, the family never owning a car, house, or going anywhere on holiday. We have access to all this now in my family life. I live a virtually middle-class lifestyle.

When I first joined the church, it was a very old-fashioned type of environment. It was not like the stone age, but I remember only two members owned and drove a car to church. There was a church van, but that was mainly for children and elders, so a lot of people (me included) took the bus or train or even rode a bicycle or, on a summer's day, walked. In the winter, I recall the church hall having to be heated by a gas heater to keep the brethren warm, but the lack of comfort was not a hindrance to faithful men and women. All were labouring together and, being almost exclusively a black organisation, very few of us could be described as educated middle-class folk. Just like a historical figure, I saw us as championing the cause of the needy, but somewhere among the subsequent affluence, we have lost the vision. Where are the labourers and soldiers that Jesus spoke of?

Where is the working church hero?

Used to think I was right,
Taking the position of the rebel.
Used to think that this fight was against the system, the elders and the Devil.
What's happening now?
I feel I'm back at zero.
Where is the working church hero?

Got to have a cause,
Worth the fussing and fighting,
E'en at early doors,
Thoughts that I found frightening.
No leaders now,
Like King or Nero.
Where is the working church hero?

Am I holding middle-class values now, And
what's the church's motto?
Be like a Joseph by the side of Pharaoh,
And revive the state of the working church hero.

A working church hero is a good thing to be.
If you're a working church hero, then you're a labourer like me.
Company-like directors the church can't afford.
If you're a working church hero, then you're following the Lord.

7.
I Need More of You

Need I say more

I need more of your love
(to help me through the bitter days)
Just give me more of your grace
(each and every day)
Just because I'm in church
(reading your word every day)
Lord, I still pray every day
Lord, I need more of you

Even though I never miss a Sunday
I still need more of you
Young men's fellowship on Mondays
I still need more of you
Even though I may be a good teacher
Maybe I am a better preacher
I still need more of you
Now I'm made assistant pastor
I still need more of you
And now this matter's not for laughter
I still need more of you

8.
Perceptions of A Christian

Sometimes people give you the big up and this can be a burden as you try and live your life by what these people think of you. It can become like a kind of Chinese whispers where words (good or bad) can be banded about and are not a true reflection of you and the subsequent perceptions of you can therefore become errant.

I guess you want to hear me say,
I woke up early, got on my knees to pray
To tell the truth, it's not the case
And this is something that I have to face

And as the day goes by, it sounds absurd
I never really got to read the word
You really want to hear me shout
About the many times I've cast a demon out

How many times have I told you this
I'm not a shrink or an Educational Psychologist
And though I'm a master of the class
In truth, I've failed as much as I have passed
I'm just the same as you
Need prayers to see me through

And as the day progresses, Oh Lord,
My Christian experiences have left me bored
If you're surprised at this, then hear
I'm often weak and trembling, full of fear
And as the night draws on with haste
It's just another day that I may waste
It's just another day that I lay chaste

How many times I've told you this
I'm not a shrink or an Educational Psychologist
And though I'm a master of the class
In truth, I've failed as much as I have passed
I'm just the same as you
Need prayers to see me through

9.
How Do You Praise the Lord?

One of the recurring pieces of advice given to me from my elders in the faith was … in all things give God thanks'. But how easy is it to do when things are not going so well? When there is no money or the job is not going very well or there is no job at all. When you are not in your good place how do you trust God? How do you perceive people who are doing so? Some have no doubt learnt to have complete trust and reliance on God's helping hand in all circumstances and all situations.

My finances are in a mess, is this just a test?
Cannot even speak to those I want to bless
Preaching not so strong, teaching is all wrong Don't feel the spirit that normally comes along So how do you praise the Lord?
So how do you praise the Lord?
So how do you praise the Lord?
So how do you praise the Lord?

'Tis God who provides the job for you to earn a bob
The blessings are from Him, not from your own gob!
Preaching may well cease, the teaching may decrease But try to remember that it is God who gives increase (So now) praise the Lord!
(So now) praise the Lord!
(So now) praise the Lord!

10.
I'm Still in God

No matter what is going on in your life someone else's life that may be close to you try remaining in God's will. There are many things we can all relate to such as disappointments, frustrations, disillusionment but there are somethings that are harder unless we are going through it ourselves or we have some issues that is comparable.

I'm still in God,
I'm glad to say.
I'm in a funny way, I give you that,
I've lost the plot.
So many times,
It makes me feel like giving up,
But I'm still in God, thank the Lord.

You're still in God,
Don't you know.
You're in desperate times, I give you that,
You've started over.
So many times,
You must be going through a torrid time,
But you're still in God, praise the Lord.

So yes, I know that you're feeling blue,
So yes, I had that feeling to.
So yes, I'll tell what you're gonna do,
Let the grace of God see you through.

11.
Prayerless Nights

Endless it seems so endless….
Are not the months of November and December the most difficult to take? These are dark cold miserable months which physically and mentally are hard to bear. I always encourage myself that after the 21st of December the days will now start getting lighter. You may not notice it but it is actually getting lighter.

They say the 21st of December
Is the longest night of all other nights,
But there was a time, I remember,
Seemed the nights were endless; I could not give you praise.

It was those prayerless nights that were the longest.

They say the river Nile in Egypt
Is a long river that flows through the land,
And I recall a time
My life meandered aimlessly through the days and weeks.

Those aimless days were the longest.

They say there is a day in the month of June,
The days are bright and there seems eternal light.

But how I bless you,
And now I thank you,
For a special time so much stronger
Make my prayerful days even longer.

12.
You Want Your Blessing (I Want Mine)

We are all looking for something better maybe or some sort of fulfilment—a blessing if you will. Some of the most humblest people I know are the ones that often give out the most and through their own challenges they ultimately become a blessing to others. So let's not be too quick to think everyone is okay apart from me myself and I as after all, we all want a blessing don't we.

You've got a troubled spirit—
Well, so have I.
Please don't assume I'm fine and make me sigh.

You've felt depression—Well, so have I.
Don't take for granted that I'm on a high.

You'll have your struggles, sis, and so will I.
I've had them for years now, and that's no lie.

You want your blessing (I want mine).

13.
Sweetly Saved (Ballerina Girl)

My very first Pastor used to reserve an expression (particularly for children and younger people) which was being 'sweetly saved.' The expression was basically her way of expressing the joy she felt when a younger person committed their ways to God. Oh the gracefulness just like a ballet dancer performing on stage beautiful to see

Isn't she sweetly saved,
As saved as one ever could be?
Suddenly, God has wrought a change in her heart.
I can't believe it; but it must be true.
I didn't think that this could happen to you (in my life).

Yes, I am sweetly saved,
As saved as the other brethren.
Suddenly, God has brought a change in my life.
I can't believe it; Lord, I feel so free.
I didn't think that this could happen to me (in your life).

But doesn't she move so well,
Just like a ballerina?
Hey, ballerina girl, you look so fine.
I can't believe; Lord, I feel so free.
I didn't think that this could happen to me.

Could that someone be you?
Ballerina girl… ballerina girl…

14.
I Will, I Must, I Can

I MUST!

I WILL ACCEPT YOUR WILL, I WILL STRIVE TO PRAY STILL, I WILL READ YOUR WORD (NOT GET BORED), I WILL PRAISE YOU, I WILL LEARN OF YOU, I WILL PERSEVERE, I WILL BE FAITHFUL IN LITTLE, I WILL KNOW MORE OF YOU, I WILL BLESS YOU, I WILL STAY HOLY, I WILL GIVE UNTO YOU, I WILL THINK ON YOU, I WILL TRUST YOU, I WILL CELEBRATE **I WIIL!** I MUST STAY SAVED, I MUST WALK WHERE JESUS PAVED, I MUST CONTINUE IN THE FAITH, I MUST BE AN EXAMPLE, I MUST REMEMBER CALVARY, I MUST HOLD FAST THAT WHICH IS GOOD, I MUST NOT FALTER (OR ALTER), I MUST NOT COMPROMISE, I MUST SAY YES TO YOUR WILL, I MUST HAVE PATIENCE **I MUST!** I CAN LIVE A CHRISTIAN LIFE, I CAN LIVE WITHOUT A WIFE, I CAN STAY FREE FROM SIN, I CAN MAKE IT IN, I CAN DO IT IN JESUS' NAME, I CAN BE A BLESSING, I CAN GIVE IT MY BEST, I CAN DO ALL THINGS THROUGH CHRIST WHO'S MY REST, I CAN BE A WINNER, I CAN BE REVIVED, I CAN BE GLORIFIED, I CAN BE SAVED, STAY SAVED, KNOW I'M SAVED.

I CAN!
I WILL! I MUST! I CAN!

15.
Running with Horses

Do you get tired with the pedestrian way of life right now? Plodding along at a snail's pace without any particular direction? Wouldn't it be great to keep pace metaphorically with a black stallion galloping through the meadow? Or maybe even physically run with a horse as Brother James once did. Wouldn't that be crazy!!

RUNNING WITH HORSES
COS IT'S SO MUCH FUN
RUNNING, WITH HORSES
LET GOD'S WILL BE DONE

JEREMIAH 12:5

I WANT TO RUN WITH HORSES
I WANT TO RUN
I WANT TO RUN WITH HORSES
COS IT'S SO MUCH FUN
I WANT TO RUN WITH HORSES
LET GOD'S WILL BE DONE
I WANT TO RUN WITH HORSES
I WANT TO RUN

RUNNING WITH HORSES YEA YEA
RUNNING WITH HORSES YEA YEA
RUNNING WITH HORSES YEA YEA

WALKING WITH THE FOOTMEN DOES N'T GET YOU NOWHERE
RUNNING WITH HORSES WITH THE LORD IS LIKE
RUNNING ON AIR

I WANT TO RUN WITH HORSES
I WANT TO RUN
I WANT TO RUN WITH HORSES
COS IT'S SO MUCH FUN
I WANT TO RUN WITH HORSES
LET GOD'S WILL BE DONE
I WANT TO RUN WITH HORSES
I WANT TO RUN

16.
Before Serving God Went Out of Style

My heart was pressing
For that next blessing
Through prayer and study
The spirit caressing
The church on fire

And our desire?

To be a light
And lift God higher

But now I'm guessing
For that next blessing
No prayer, no study
Freedoms we're stressing
And now there's no fire
What's our desire?
We say we're in light
We make him a liar

I'm glad I've tasted
And haven't wasted
The grace of your saving
For souls, I'm still craving
Though grace was often a trial
Before serving God went out of style

I'm sad for others
Who haven't bothered
To stop all the messing
And experience true blessings

Though in truth I haven't had this feeling for a while
Since serving God went out of style
(But it's going to come back into fashion it's going to come back into fashion)

17.
Listen to the Spirit Song

Ah, National Church Convention by the sea, what memories that come flooding back. It always seemed to be sunny, there always seemed to be an almost carnival-like atmosphere when we marched, everybody seemed to be upbeat and colourful and… but enough of nostalgia! This particular convention morning, I got to say, was cold, chilly & nobody was about, but I went down to the beach to be alone with God and let him minister to me through the sea, sand, and seagulls…

In the early morn,
I got that new-born
Feeling of your presence
Seagulls I hear,
Nothing to fear,
Getting closer to your presence.
Out of sight,
Out of mind,
Out of this world,
Feeling of your presence.

Feel so good, I almost could… Listen to the spirit song.
Feel so good, I almost should… Listen to the spirit song.
Feel so good, I almost would… Listen to the spirit song.

18.
I've Seen a Rainbow

What is a rainbow? Is it just something that happens after heavy rain and then some sunshine? Or is there something more heavenly that we can learn from such an occurrence.

I've seen a rainbow,
It reminds me of you.
I've seen a rainbow,
Gives me confidence in you.
So I'm writing these words
To encourage one like you.
Remember the rainbow,
It's God's everlasting promise to you.

I've seen a rainbow,
It makes me feel nice.
So when I get the blues,
I'm gonna think twice,
Keep the feeling on ice.
It's God's everlasting promise to you.

Brother Richard O' York,
Gaining battles in vain.
You should know that for rainbows,
Sun comes after the rain.
That clearly is plain.
It's God's everlasting promise to you.

19.
We're Not Together Now

Have we lost that deep relationship that we once had with each other? Any relationship, brother, sister, parent, child, husband, wife needs working on. I read somewhere that the family that prays together stays together but is this always true?

Let us pull, pull, pull altogether,
Let us pray, pray, pray altogether,
'Cos there is coming a time when we all shall be together.
So let's get together now.

I'd like to know where we are going to go.
My feelings are scrambled,
And your life in shambles.

At first, it was great, even though you were late.
And I was elated, even though sometimes frustrated.
But you couldn't see what was happening to me,
And we're not together now.

You couldn't deal with the feelings you feel,
Though I got it wrong 'cos my feelings were strong.
And I didn't know how to go with this flow,
Since we're not together now.

I told you each day that we both should pray,
The games Satan plays in so many ways.
And we got annoyed as the enemy toyed,
And knew we weren't together now.

Let us pull, pull, pull altogether,
Let us pray, pray, pray altogether,
'Cos there is coming a time when we all shall be together.
So, let's get together now.

20.
She Prays She Prays She Prays

There are some bothers (mainly sisters) that really could pray. I mean they could pray! One hour—still going, two hours—still going, three hours etc. etc. Praying next to them made you feel inadequate. These types of sisters we would call 'Prayer Warriors' due to the aggressive nature of some of their prayers as if they were going to battle with enemy forces in the spiritual realm

She prays… for the Church of God

She prays for everyone early in the morning,
She prays for everyone, EVERYONE,
She prays for everyone before the sun is dawning,
She prays for everyone, EVERYONE,
She prays for everyone, EVERYONE.

She prays for all the little children to be saved,
For all teenagers to be delivered from raves.
She prays for everyone; she prays for everyone.

She prays, 'Let God's will be done',
She prays, 'Thy kingdom come',
She prays, 'Let God's will be done', She prays, 'Thy kingdom come'.

She prays, She prays, She prays.

21.
Don't Pray Me Down Too Soon!

My first ever Pastor, before she began to share the sermon would say this. I want you to pray me up then I want you to pray me down but don't pray me down too soon. So Pastor Elizabeth C. Wiltshire ... I wont

You Pray me up, You pray me down,
You Pray me up, down, all around.
Any way you feel, that's fine,
Any way you pray me, that's fine.
But when I'm preaching Jesus brother,
Don't pray me down too soon.

You Pray me North, You pray me South,
You Pray me North, South, East, West.
Any way you feel, that's the best,
Any way you pray me, I'm blessed.
But when I'm preaching Jesus, sister,
Don't pray me down too soon.

Don't pray me down (don't pray me down),
Don't pray me down (don't pray me down),
Don't pray me down (don't pray me down),
Don't pray me down too soon.

22.
I'm Not Satisfied

Brother Keith is not the only one looking for satisfaction in life, I guess we all are in some shape or form. I try and balance the insatiable quest for more and more by this scripture found I Timothy 6:6.
But godliness with contentment is great gain

I'm not satisfied at all with…
Living beneath my privilege with…
Fighting for my blessing with… Striving for The Grace.
I want to meet the Lord face to face and say, I'm not satisfied.

I'm not satisfied at all with…
The way that we all are living with… Talking and talking and talking with… Living on the edge of a knife. I want a change in my life because I'm not satisfied.

23.
It's Only Prayer

Sometimes we spend so much energy talking, shouting, debating, trying to prove we are right and you are wrong and for what? Even talking with friends or professionals can cause more harm than good. It is not always the case that a problem shared is a problem halved. So why is talking to God often the last port of call even for the seasoned Christian? Why has talking about prayer, theorising about prayer, singing about prayer and even texting about prayer become a substitute for actually praying? After all is said and done—it's only prayer.

It's only prayer, my my,
It's only prayer, so why why,
Am I struggling with it, sigh sigh?
It's only prayer.

Please don't get me wrong,
But to sing a song,
As I play along,
Is not as strong
As a life of prayer.

Please, I can't believe
That you're trying to tease
And remain deceived,
While we all appease
The lack of prayer.

It's only prayer, my my,
It's only prayer, so why why,
Am I struggling with it, sigh sigh?
It's only prayer.

24.
Pray for Yourself

I am not talking about the egotistical prayer where one only cares about oneself but rather the mature believer who has passed the stage of draining individuals with the constant need for prayer without ever giving anything back. Got to get beyond the place of praying FOR me and reach the place of praying WITH me.

Praying will see you thru
If you know who you're praying to
Pray for yourself cos I can't pray for you

It may sound crazy
But I can't pray for you as I'm in need of prayer for me
No ifs or maybes
Cos if you don't try prayer this may cause you more misery
Praying will see you thru
If you know who you're praying to
Pray for yourself cos I won't pray for you

It might be lazy
But I can't pray for you as I'm in need of prayer for me
No ifs or maybes
Cos if you don't try prayer we'll never set our spirit free
Praying will see you thru
If know who you're praying to
Pray for yourself cos God will be there for you
(You've got to) do what you gotta do
(And you should) know who you're praying to
Pray for yourself Cos God will be there for you
Pray for yourself Cos God will be there for you

25.
Frustration

Need I Say More. What frustrates you? Bad manners, queue jumpers, children, your spouse, (your lack of spouse?), church God…

I am trying hard to serve the Lord whilst I am still alive,
But I'm finding it a struggle; please help me, Jesus, to survive. Yes, I'm praying, yes, I'm fasting, but I feel no change within. If this is the case, then what's the point of telling me 'refrain from sin?'
Why don't people understand I like to serve my Master and my King.
Why do I have to explain almost every little thing?

I'm trying, I'm trying.

Why do brethren always seem to still turn up late?
If this was heaven, we'd be outside those sweet pearly gates.
Why have I been serving Jesus? I have been serving Him for many years.
Lord, give me the love and power that takes away all of my fears.
Why do others think I have the answer to their every need?
On the contrary, don't you know that Jesus said to you,
"These lambs, please feed?"

Frustration, Frustration.

Why don't people grow and mature and be a blessing to the church?
Why do people stay undeveloped and leave the gospel in the lurch?
Yes, I feel I need to grow and grow to be of service to the Lord,
But I am prevented by some brethren; of this, I really cannot afford.

Frustration, Frustration.

26.
Are You, My Friend?

How can we have friendship with that which is divine? What are the boundaries? Can good qualities such as wisdom, knowledge understanding be personified into something relational? Can God look down after speaking with the heavenly host and declare like Job that I am a friend?

Are You My Friend?
Are You My Friend?
Are You My Friend?

Lord are you my friend are you my not Friend?
Where did this start where does this end?
Is this a one off or some kind of trend?
I want to know lord are you my Friend?

27.
Playing Church?

When I was a child, I spoke as a child, I understood as a child, I reasoned as a child. Have you ever reminisced on past (non) misspent youth? If the Bible teaches me that man's life is three score and ten (70), then boy, I am well into the second half of my life already! Time to get serious about my life. I am really impressed also with those faithful ministers who have laboured in challenging areas such as children's ministries, Sunday School, and Youth Ministries. The phrase 'playing church' was often used by elders to denote that we should be mature and grown up about our Christian faith. Playing church was also something we as younger ones did when we were trying to imitate our elders' preaching and teaching style.

When we were children,
I was the preacher,
You were the teacher,
Oh, what a time!
Now we're older, older and wiser,
Are you still teaching?
All of the time.

When we were teens,
I was the youth leader,
You were in children's ministries,
Oh, what a time!
Now we're older, older and wiser,
Are you still with children,
All of the time.

Now I'm in adulthood,
I am a Pastor,
You are a Pastor,
Where is the time?
As we are older, surely we're wiser,
To handle the problems,
All of the time.

Hey, Sister Annie,
What are you doing now?
Are you still playing church?
Hey, Sister Annie,
What are you doing now?
Are you still playing church?
Now we're older, older and wiser,
Are you still teaching,
All of the time?
Are you still playing church?
Are you still playing church?…

28.
You're My Blessed Friend

Someone once told me that she did not have many friends but the few that she had were real quality. In this present time, people boast about how many followers they have on a blog or website but what about friendship fellowship? What we need are those close associations that we can call in real moments of need. We don't even need best friends but so much but maybe we need some blessed friends.

When I was a young teenager,
You were a friend I looked up to.
I had a starry-eyed face,
Couldn't you trace
That I wished I was like you in so many ways?
You're my blessed friend.

When I was learning the guitar,
You were a friend I could learn from.
I wanted you to see
The music in me,
But I wished I could play guitar like you.
You're my blessed friend.

When I was a hungry young student,
You were a teacher most humble
You taught the Hebrew, the Greek,
More knowledge I would seek,
But I couldn't get enough of what you had to give.
You're my blessed friend.

Ooh, I've been blessed beyond measure,
Maybe there's more I can gain from you.
Ooh, I've been blessed beyond measure,
Maybe there's something I can offer you to Ooh, you're my blessed friend.
You're my blessed friend.

29.
One in A Million

What's the probability of winning the lottery? Or finding life on Mars? I guess a million to one. Do you know the probability of you being born is literally one in a million? Well, that's a fact. The scripture also tells us that the Father knows every hair on our head is numbered (possibly a million). Well, is that a fact? Every day, 70 to 150 million sperm is released, but only one can make it to the egg to make a baby and, with those odds, it is a miracle we are here. The Psalmist David (or the saxophonist David?) realised the unique and miraculous nature of mankind, so when we think we are nothing—we actually [are] one in a million.

I'm one in a million and I'm grateful to God for this feeling,
Once I didn't really think it appealing,
Until your word, so revealing,
Told me I'm one in a million.

You're one in a million and don't you forget it,
So there's no need to regret it.
You realise this if you let it,
That you're one in a million.

You're one in a million—a million-to-one shot,
Although you may not feel as hot as you once did,
I'll tell you this to be sure,
I'll tell you this much once more,
You're one in a million to God,
You're one in a million to God,
You're one in a million to God.

30.
(No Morning Glory) What's the Story?

One of my more touchy moments. At a regional gathering, I was to play the part of the runner, cleaner, dishwasher, and any other kitchen requirements for the benefit of 1000 people who were enjoying the church meeting—God, it was hard work! As a result, I would hear no messages, no teaching, no nothing. Each morning, the meeting would start with a session called Morning Glory, which was basically an oasis of singing praise and prayer. No morning glory for me, Brother Noel.

No morning glory? What's the story?
I'm in this here kitchen.
What's the game? In Jesus' name?
I'm in this here kitchen.

I can't figure out the reason
Why I am so far from you, Lord?
So I wash up all the dishes,
Hoping you'll come through.

31.
Prayer Walking

Have you ever been on a prayer walk? You should try it; it is good fun, even in the confines of your own home, but it is better outside. You can do it alone or with other people, when it sounds like a mini army marching and praying through an area. It's a great way also to keep fit and stay alive, as Brother G will testify.

Pray walk! Pray Walk! Pray Walk! Pray Walk!

Prayer walking is keeping you sane,
Prayer walking again and again.
'Cos when you and God start talking,
No problems remain.
And when you're through prayer walking, you're winning again.

32.
Yes, No, Wait

Have we understood the three ways God answers prayer? Yes No and Wait. We all feel really good when the answers are Yes but can we exercise patience when God says wait? Or do we act like petulant children when the answer is a resounding NO! Waiting does not mean that we do not actively engage in other issues until that which we are waiting on comes to pass. In conclusion, No does not mean never

I've always wondered why
Despite the tears I cry,
I am the same, and time has flown.
The frustration that I feel,
The wounds that will not heal,
It's the worst I've ever known.

Believe me when I say,
I've tried really hard to pray
I've tried really hard to pray.
It's always yes, no, wait

I guess you feel the same.
Is this a crazy game
That the Lord will put us through?
I feel you ought to know
He's seen it all before,
So that there's nothing here that's new

Believe me when I say
Jesus will show you the way
Jesus will show you the way
He'll answer yes no wait
Yes, Lord, I want to believe it and…
No doesn't mean I'll never receive it and I'll…
Wait on the Lord to achieve it for all of life.

33.
You Don't Know Me

The Johari Window is a model that was designed to help us better understand ourselves and others. It teaches us that there are four main areas: The Arena, known to us and others; the blind spot, known to others but not to us; the façade, not known to others but known to us; and the unknown, not known to either ourselves or others. I would like to take the liberty of renaming this as the 'God Only Knows' area, as in truth, not only do you not know me, but I don't even know myself. As Brother Brian said, God Only Knows.

I've been knowing you for oh, so long,
And for all these years as we sing our song.
And you know so well the things that I like to say,
And you know so well the things that I like to pray,
And you know so well the things that I like to play.
But I have news for you,
Think you know it to
You don't know me,
You don't know me.

I have been open to you for many years,
And for weeks on end, you have heard my prayers.
And you know so well the things that I like to say,
And you know so well the things that I like to pray,
And you know so well the things that I like to play.
For when we cut to the chase,
Though we meet face to face,
You don't know me,
You don't know me.

Are you blind, or am I, that we cannot see?
Take off all the layers, and is this the real me?
And you know so well the things that I like to say,
And you know so well the things that I like to pray,
And you know so well the things that I like to play.
At the end of the day,
I'll say this if I may,
You don't know me,
You don't know me.

Why do you think that I cannot sing?
Why do you think that I can't wear an earring?
Why, if I plait my hair, would you stare?
Why do you think that I should always be here?

Want to tell you more, but it's really hard,
Want to show you that there is no façade.
And you know so well the things that I like to say,
And you know so well the things that I like to pray,
And you know so well the things that I like to play.
Even if I shout,
No, please hear me out,
You don't know me,
You don't know me.

Why do you think that I cannot sing?
Why do you think that I can't wear an earring?
Why, if I plait my hair, would you stare?
Why do you think that I should always be here?

34.
They Came in Through the Church Back Window

At a church in Bedford, there were three young travellers that attended the church one Sunday morning and stole some items and money from the church. They had said their goodbyes but sneaked back in when most, if not all, the congregation had gone downstairs to share a meal. Being the father of the child who had his iPad stolen, I was naturally quite annoyed and could not understand why they could not have been more up front and ask for money, clothes, or food if they needed this? There is a deeper thought, however, which is based on the believers' moving away from the verse found in St John 10:1. Have we been seeking alternative entry points to the Kingdom rather than coming through the 'door' Jesus. Are we therefore as bad as those three traveller boys?

They came in through the church back window,
Right before my very eyes.
They did not leave the church an offering,
They did not leave the church some tithes.

The usher told them of their error,
In so many loving words,
"No need to come in through the window."
But I wonder if they even heard.

Didn't anybody teach you?
Didn't anybody care?
Sunday morning after service,
There is a meal that we all can share.

So if you want to go to heaven,
And not to go down to hell,
You've got to know Jesus is the door,
That you should know very well.

They came in through the church back window,
The congregation must have heard (no, they didn't!)
They did not listen to the preacher,
They did not listen to the word.

Didn't anybody tell you?
Didn't anybody share much more?
Jesus is the way to heaven,
And He is knocking at your door.

35.
Gimme Wisdom

Are our lives becoming one of gimme, gimme, gimme? Rather than thank you, thank you, thank you? No appreciation for what we have and demanding more of what we have in abundance? Nothing wrong with having nice things but let's ask God for wisdom on what we acquire and how it is used.

I don't need more material goods, I am content, I am not that vain.
I don't need more money, as godliness with contentment is great gain.
Brother Michael, I don't need shelter, I have been blessed with a place to live.
Although it's not a mansion, I know to God the thanks I give.
So Abba Father does not need to find a man before or after midnight.
Please, God, just gimme wisdom and I'm sure I'll be alright.

Oooh there's, there's a blessing… It's just a prayer away, it's just a prayer away.
Oooh there's, there's a blessing… Gimme wisdom for the day.

Gimme wisdom,
Can't you hear me say?
I need it every day,
I need it, Lord, I pray,
Gimme wisdom.

Gimme wisdom,
I need it in the school,
So I don't act the fool,
So I can play it cool,
Lord, gimme wisdom

If you want wisdom,
You need to come to me,
I give it liberally.
If you want wisdom,
You only need to ask,
And I will do the task.

I don't need another pair of shoes,
The ones I have got are just fine.
No need for more Reebok, Nike, or Adidas,
You can only wear one pair at a time!

Sister, you don't need a new dress,
Or a fancy new hat,
Just let the Lord's righteousness clothe you,
And be satisfied with that!

Oooh, there's a blessing… It's just a prayer away, it's just a prayer away.
Oooh, there's a blessing… Gimme wisdom for the day.